Building Spelling Skills
Grade 4
Daily Practice

Spelling Strategies

Building Spelling Skills

Say a word correctly.

- Don't leave out or mispronounce sounds.
- Write the sounds in the correct order.

Think about what the word looks like.

- Think about how the spelling pattern looks.
- Write it, look at it, and decide if it looks correct.

Look for small words in spelling words.

- spin—**pin, in**
- cupcake—**cup, cake**

Look at syllables in spelling words.

- Spell the word one syllable at a time.
  remember—**re • mem • ber**

Use rhyming words to help spell a word.

- If you can spell **book**, you can spell **look**.

Use rules for adding endings.

- Drop silent **e** before adding a suffix.
- Double the final consonant before adding a suffix.
- Change the final **y** to **i** and add **es**.

These strategies help me become a better speller!

How to Study Your List

Building Spelling Skills

1 Read and Spell

2 Copy and Spell

3 Cover and Spell

4 Uncover and Check

Good for me!

Building Spelling Skills

WEEK 1

Spelling List

This Week's Focus:
- Spell words with consonant blends
- Spell two-syllable words

STEP 1 Read and Spell

1. bridge
2. gravity
3. hungry
4. eclipse
5. secret
6. applaud
7. laundry
8. trouble
9. attract
10. twilight
11. between
12. describe
13. snowflake
14. freedom
15. slimy
16. glance
17. burglar
18. switch
19. _____ bonus word
20. _____ bonus word

STEP 2 Copy and Spell

bridge bridge
gravity gravity
hungry hungry
eclipse eclipse
secret secret
applaud applaud
laundry Laundry
trouble trouble
attract attract
twilight twilight
between between
describe describe
snowflake Snowflake
freedom freedom
slimy slimy
glance glance
burglar burglar
switch switch.

STEP 3 Cover and Spell

Building Spelling Skills, Daily Practice • EMC 6684 © Evan-Moor Corporation

Word Meaning

Building Spelling Skills — WEEK 1

Fill in the blanks.

bridge	gravity	hungry	eclipse	between
trouble	attract	laundry	twilight	snowflake
freedom	slimy	glance	burglar	switch

1. The _____ lost his _____ when he was sent to jail.

2. Did you see the _____ of the sun?

3. The _____ was pretty to look at before it melted.

4. The boy was so _____ that he ate _____ meals.

5. White flowers _____ moths after _____.

6. She took one _____ at the _____ worm and screamed.

7. I had so many dirty clothes that I had _____ finishing my _____ in time for the party.

My Spelling Dictation

Write the sentences. Circle the spelling words.

1. I have a trouble, my Mom told me to cleaned the laundry but I forgot!

2. I slimy on my bed.

Word Study

Building Spelling Skills — WEEK 1

Fill in the missing letters to make spelling words.

> br　gr　tr　tw　fr　gl　sw　sn

1. bur__gl__ar
2. _____ance
3. _____ouble
4. _____avity
5. hun_____y
6. _____ilight
7. _____eedom
8. _____idge
9. at_____act
10. be_____een
11. _____owflake
12. _____itch

Circle the words with the sound of **e** as in **we**.
Underline the words that have a silent **e** as in **make**.

glance	freedom	snowflake	between
trouble	secret	eclipse	bridge

Match syllables to make spelling words.
Write the complete words on the lines.

1. hun — gry
2. se — cret
3. laun — ble
4. trou — light
5. twi — dry
6. be — dom
7. snow — flake
8. free — tween

1. ____hungry____
2. _____
3. _____
4. _____
5. _____
6. _____
7. _____
8. _____

Edit for Spelling

Building Spelling Skills — WEEK 1

Circle the word in each row that is spelled correctly.

1. freedom   fredom   freedum   ferdom
2. betwen   between   beetwen   betwin
3. twiliht   tylight   twilight   twilite
4. atract   attract   attracte   attrat
5. trouble   truble   troubl   troubel
6. applad   applaude   applawd   applaud
7. bredge   bridg   bridge   brige
8. secrat   secret   seecret   secrit

Circle the misspelled words in the sentences.
Write them correctly on the lines.

1. One glanc at the food and I was hugry.
   _____ _____

2. Would you like to swich to a new lawndry soap?
   _____ _____

3. Please dascribe the slimee bug.
   _____ _____

4. Gravety pulled the snoflak to the ground.
   _____ _____

5. The burgler was caught during an eclips of the sun.
   _____ _____

Building Spelling Skills

WEEK 2

Spelling List

This Week's Focus:
- Spell words with consonant digraphs spelled **th**, **ch**, **tch**, and **wh**
- Spell words with the /ər/ sound spelled **er** and **ir**
- Spell words that begin with **spr** and **thr**

STEP 1 Read and Spell

STEP 2 Copy and Spell

STEP 3 Cover and Spell

1. attach
2. where
3. sandwich
4. change
5. watch
6. singer
7. slippery
8. spring
9. gather
10. these
11. thread
12. athlete
13. worth
14. thirsty
15. whisper
16. whistle
17. awhile
18. nowhere
19. _____ bonus word
20. _____ bonus word

Word Meaning

Building Spelling Skills — WEEK 2

Fill in the blanks.

1. Do you know _____ (where, nowhere) he put the bottle of _____ (spring, these) water?

2. The _____ (worth, athlete) wanted to rest _____ (awhile, nowhere).

3. Blow your _____ (whisper, whistle) and have the students _____ (attach, gather) by the flagpole.

4. Would you please _____ (watch, where) _____ (nowhere, these) children?

5. I don't like peanut butter. May I _____ (attach, change) my _____ (thread, sandwich)?

6. The _____ (worth, singer) performs the song in a _____ (whisper, nowhere).

7. He was _____ (attach, thirsty), but there was _____ (nowhere, where) in the desert to get a drink.

8. The slide isn't _____ (worth, attach) much if it isn't _____ (slippery, thread).

My Spelling Dictation

Write the sentences. Circle the spelling words.

1. _____

_____

2. _____

_____

Word Study

Building Spelling Skills — WEEK 2

Answer the questions using spelling words.

1. Which words contain the digraph **th**?
   Circle every **th** that has the sound you hear in **thin** or **the**.

   __(th)ese__   _____   _____

   _____   _____   _____

2. Which words contain the digraph **ch**?
   Circle every **ch** that has the sound you hear in **chin**.

   _____   _____   _____

3. Which word contains the digraph **tch**?
   Circle the **tch** that has the sound you hear in **catch**.

   _____

4. Which words contain the digraph **wh**?

   _____   _____   _____

   _____   _____

Fill in the missing digraphs to make spelling words.

(th   ch   tch   wh)

1. no____ere
2. ____irsty
3. wa____
4. ____ere
5. atta____
6. a____ile
7. wor____
8. ga____er
9. ____ange
10. ____ese
11. ____read
12. ____isper
13. sandwi____
14. a____lete
15. ____istle

Edit for Spelling

Building Spelling Skills — WEEK 2

Underline the words that are spelled correctly.

sandwitch	singor	slippery
worth	awile	thes
spring	wisper	nowhere
wach	whistle	thursty

Circle the misspelled words in the sentences.
Write them correctly on the lines.

1. Atach a note to the sack containing the sandwech.
   _____   _____

2. The athle was thirsdy.
   _____   _____

3. Everyone wached the singr.
   _____   _____

4. Please whispor awile before the play begins.
   _____   _____

5. No where are seashells wurth more than here.
   _____   _____

6. I like to whistel when winter changs to spring.
   _____   _____

Building Spelling Skills

WEEK 3

Spelling List

This Week's Focus:
- Spell words with the short **a** sound
- Spell words with the long **a** sound spelled **a**, **ai**, **ay**, **eigh**, and **ei**

STEP 1 Read and Spell

1. fact
2. began
3. clasp
4. rapid
5. able
6. later
7. space
8. stranger
9. grade
10. display
11. main
12. explain
13. freight
14. neighbor
15. weigh
16. vein
17. April
18. ankle
19. _____ bonus word
20. _____ bonus word

STEP 2 Copy and Spell

STEP 3 Cover and Spell

Building Spelling Skills, Daily Practice • EMC 6684

Word Meaning

Building Spelling Skills — WEEK 3

Fill in the blanks.

> able space stranger grade display
> explain neighbor weigh April ankle

1. I'm in the fourth _____ at school.

2. My next-door _____ moved in during the month of _____.

3. My mom says to never talk to a _____.

4. Let me _____ why I want to borrow a dollar.

5. I hurt my _____, but I'm _____ to walk on it.

6. I _____ 60 pounds.

7. I will put my dog on _____ at the next dog show.

8. My dentist said I didn't have enough _____ between my teeth.

My Spelling Dictation

Write the sentences. Circle the spelling words.

1. _____

   _____

   _____

2. _____

   _____

   _____

Word Study

Building Spelling Skills — WEEK 3

List the spelling words with the sound of long **a**.
Then circle the letters that make the long **a** sound. Circle the letters **a**, **ai**, **ay**, **ei**, or **eigh**.

1. _explain_ (ai circled)
2. _____
3. _____
4. _____
5. _____
6. _____
7. _____
8. _____
9. _____
10. _____
11. _____
12. _____
13. _____

List the spelling words with the sound of short **a**. Then circle the letters that make the short **a** sound.

1. _____
2. _____
3. _____
4. _____
5. _____

Match syllables to make words. Write the complete word on the line.

1. neigh   play   1. _____
2. dis   bor   2. _____
3. be   ger   3. _____
4. ex   id   4. _____
5. stran   gan   5. _____
6. rap   plain   6. _____

Building Spelling Skills, Daily Practice • EMC 6684 © Evan-Moor Corporation

Edit for Spelling

Building Spelling Skills — WEEK 3

Circle the 15 misspelled words in the story below. Write them correctly on the lines.

April's Space Report

April wrote a report and made a dicplay about spac. Her report begain with many facs. She explained how much a person would weighe on the moon, the rapide speed of light, and even strangor things. Her display had one mane feature, a picture of the freigt the space shuttle carries.

All of Apirl's hard work was rewarded. Her project was given an A grad. Latter that afternoon, April showed her project to her naighbor. Her nayhbor gave April a big hug.

_____   _____

_____   _____

_____   _____

_____   _____

_____   _____

_____   _____

_____   _____

_____

Building Spelling Skills

WEEK 4

Spelling List

This Week's Focus:
- Spell words with the short e sound
- Spell words with the long e sound spelled ea, ee, ei, ie, e, and eo

STEP 1 Read and Spell

1. then
2. else
3. edge
4. when
5. tenth
6. empty
7. sketch
8. spelling
9. easy
10. eager
11. sneakers
12. mean
13. fifteen
14. receive
15. piece
16. believe
17. people
18. squeeze
19. _____ bonus word
20. _____ bonus word

STEP 2 Copy and Spell

STEP 3 Cover and Spell

Word Meaning

Building Spelling Skills — WEEK 4

Fill in the blanks with spelling words.

else	when	tenth	empty
sketch	easy	eager	sneakers
mean	fifteen	receive	piece
believe	spelling	people	squeeze

1. Fred tried to _____ all the juice out of the _____ of fruit.

2. What _____ could the _____ do but laugh?

3. There were _____ runners in the race. Frederica came in _____.

4. How many _____ words do you _____ you can spell correctly?

5. Does the _____ bag _____ that someone took our lunch?

6. Fred was always _____ to _____ pictures in art class.

7. The athlete found running _____ when she wore _____.

8. _____ will you _____ the letter?

My Spelling Dictation

Write the sentences. Circle the spelling words.

1. _____

   _____

2. _____

   _____

Word Study

Building Spelling Skills — WEEK 4

Underline the words with the long **e** sound.
Circle the letters that make the long **e** sound. Circle the letters **e, ee, ie, ea, ei, eo,** or **y**.

1. squeeze
2. else
3. believe
4. when
5. tenth
6. sneakers
7. sketch
8. easy
9. eager
10. empty
11. mean
12. fifteen
13. receive
14. piece
15. edge
16. spelling
17. people
18. then

Underline the words with the same vowel sound you hear in **bed**.
Circle the letter that makes that sound.

1. when
2. mean
3. believe
4. piece
5. empty
6. edge
7. sketch
8. spelling
9. receive
10. tenth
11. else
12. fifteen
13. eager
14. squeeze
15. sneakers
16. easy
17. people
18. then

Write the correct spelling for the long **e** sound in these words. Write **ie** or **ei**.

bel____ve   rec____ve   p____ce

Write the spelling words that mean about the same as these words.

1. grip _____
2. enthusiastic _____
3. part _____
4. void _____
5. get _____
6. unkind _____
7. trust _____
8. drawing _____
9. border _____
10. effortless _____

Building Spelling Skills, Daily Practice • EMC 6684   © Evan-Moor Corporation

Edit for Spelling

Building Spelling Skills — WEEK 4

Circle the word in each row that is spelled correctly.

1. beleive   believ   believe   beleev
2. peice   piece   piec   pece
3. receive   recieve   reciev   resieve
4. eles   else   alse   ellse
5. easy   easee   esy   eazy
6. scetch   skech   skecth   sketch
7. imty   emty   empty   emptey
8. meen   mean   mene   meane
9. squeze   squeez   squeeze   skweez
10. spelling   speling   spellin   speleling
11. peaple   people   peple   peopel
12. eager   eger   eagar   aeger

Circle the misspelled words in the sentences. Write them correctly on the lines.

1. I was the tanth in a line of fifeteen peple.

   _____ _____ _____

2. My sneekers got wet. Than my socks got wet.

   _____ _____

3. Whin did you want to play at my house?

   _____

4. Do you know what els will happen if you stand too close to the edg?

   _____ _____

Building Spelling Skills

WEEK 5

Spelling List

This Week's Focus:
- Spell words with the short **i** sound
- Spell words with the long **i** sound spelled **i**, **y**, **igh**, and **uy**

STEP 1 Read and Spell

1. since
2. which
3. inch
4. string
5. picnic
6. shrimp
7. title
8. mind
9. wild
10. decide
11. why
12. skyscraper
13. buy
14. right
15. lightning
16. write
17. cypress
18. bicycle
19. _____ bonus word
20. _____ bonus word

STEP 2 Copy and Spell

STEP 3 Cover and Spell

Word Meaning

Complete the crossword puzzle using spelling words.

Down

1. to purchase
2. the name of a book
3. _____ one?
5. a thin rope; cord
6. an outdoor meal
9. not tame

Across

3. a question word
4. a measurement
5. a building
7. to make up your mind
8. from then until now
9. to put words on paper
10. correct

My Spelling Dictation

Write the sentences. Circle the spelling words.

1. _____

2. _____

Word Study

Building Spelling Skills — WEEK 5

Write the spelling words in the correct column.

mind	bicycle	shrimp	title	decide
inch	which	since	wild	cypress
why	skyscraper	buy	string	
picnic	lightning	write	right	

i as in fix

_____
_____
_____
_____
_____
_____
_____

i as in pie

_____
_____
_____
_____
_____
_____
_____
_____
_____
_____
_____

Match syllables to make words. Write the complete words on the lines.

1. ti   cide   1. _____
2. pic   ning   2. _____
3. de   tle   3. _____
4. light   nic   4. _____
5. cy   press   5. _____

Edit for Spelling

Building Spelling Skills WEEK 5

Circle the word in each row that is spelled correctly.

1. sens   cince   since   senc
2. writ   write   rite   rwrit
3. string   streng   strin   streg
4. titl   titel   tittle   title

Circle the 11 misspelled words below.
Write them correctly on the lines.

One Bad Picnic

The picnc was wilde. Wy, you ask? First, my bicyle had a flat on the way there. Second, there was liting and an inc of rain on the ground. Third, I couldn't dicide whitch to eat, shremp or fish. Fourth, a skiscraper blocked the sun. Finally, a cipress tree fell on our table.

_____ _____

_____ _____

_____ _____

_____ _____

_____

Building Spelling Skills

WEEK 6

Spelling List

This Week's Focus:
- Spell words with the short o sound
- Spell words with the long o sound spelled o, ow, oa, ou, and oe

STEP 1 Read and Spell

1. strong
2. wrong
3. copy
4. cloth
5. problem
6. bottom
7. whole
8. explode
9. control
10. shown
11. bowl
12. October
13. smoky
14. coach
15. throat
16. toast
17. doughnut
18. foe
19. _____ bonus word
20. _____ bonus word

STEP 2 Copy and Spell

STEP 3 Cover and Spell

Word Meaning

Building Spelling Skills — WEEK 6

Answer the questions using spelling words.

1. Which spelling word is the antonym for…?

    a. weak _____   e. solution _____

    b. part _____   f. right _____

    c. give freedom _____   g. top _____

    d. do differently _____   h. friend _____

2. What do you call…?

    a. a month in the fall _____

    b. an object that holds breakfast cereal _____

    c. a pastry with a hole in it _____

    d. warm, browned bread _____

    e. material for making clothes _____

    f. the part of the body food goes down _____

    g. a person who teaches soccer _____

My Spelling Dictation

Write the sentences. Circle the spelling words.

1. _____

_____

2. _____

_____

Word Study

Write the spelling words in the correct column.

strong	foe	wrong	doughnut
throat	toast	coach	cloth
problem	copy	smoky	whole
explode	shown	bowl	bottom

o as in fox

_____
_____
_____
_____
_____
_____

o as in hope

_____
_____
_____
_____
_____
_____
_____
_____
_____
_____

Circle the silent letter or letters in each word.

| wrong | whole | shown | bowl |
| explode | doughnut | foe | throat |

Edit for Spelling

Building Spelling Skills — WEEK 6

Circle the misspelled words in the sentences.
Write them correctly on the lines.

1. I enjoy eating a donat on a cold octobr morning.

   _____ _____

2. What went rong with the strang rope?

   _____ _____

3. Copee that probelm.

   _____ _____

4. I was shoan where to put my boal.

   _____ _____

5. The coch car on the train was too smokey.

   _____ _____

6. Are you a friend or fo?

   _____

7. The tost got stuck in my throt.

   _____ _____

8. The hole battom of my pants got wet.

   _____ _____

9. I watched the fireworks explod.

   _____

Building Spelling Skills

WEEK 7

Spelling List

This Week's Focus:
- Spell words with the short **u** sound
- Spell words with the long **u** sound spelled **ue**, **u**, and **eau**

STEP 1 Read and Spell

1. blush
2. crutch
3. crunch
4. grumpy
5. much
6. umpire
7. uncle
8. none
9. does
10. fuel
11. cute
12. cubicle
13. human
14. future
15. usual
16. uniform
17. used
18. beautiful
19. _____ bonus word
20. _____ bonus word

STEP 2 Copy and Spell

STEP 3 Cover and Spell

Word Meaning

Building Spelling Skills — WEEK 7

Write the letter of the meaning on the line in front of the spelling word.

_____	1. blush	a.	to grind or chew
_____	2. crutch	b.	irritable
_____	3. crunch	c.	to turn pink
_____	4. grumpy	d.	a parent's brother
_____	5. much	e.	zero
_____	6. umpire	f.	a person
_____	7. uncle	g.	the time ahead
_____	8. none	h.	many in number
_____	9. does	i.	a sports judge
_____	10. fuel	j.	common
_____	11. cute	k.	performs an action
_____	12. cubicle	l.	adorable
_____	13. human	m.	a small space
_____	14. future	n.	a support
_____	15. usual	o.	an energy source

My Spelling Dictation

Write the sentences. Circle the spelling words.

1. _____

2. _____

Word Study

Building Spelling Skills — WEEK 7

Write the spelling words in the correct column.

blush	uniform	usual	crutch
crunch	human	grumpy	cubicle
cute	much	fuel	uncle
umpire	none	does	used

u as in cup

_____
_____
_____
_____
_____
_____
_____
_____

u as in use

_____
_____
_____
_____
_____
_____
_____
_____

Match syllables to make spelling words.
Write the complete words on the lines.

1. grum   ture   _____
2. um   man   _____
3. hu   cle   _____
4. un   pire   _____
5. fu   py   _____

6. beau   u   ful   _____
7. un   i   al   _____
8. us   i   cle   _____
9. cub   ti   form   _____

Edit for Spelling

Building Spelling Skills — WEEK 7

Circle the 12 misspelled words below.
Write them correctly on the lines.

Soccer Is a Wonderful Game

Unless…

Your uncl says your unifurm is cut.

There's no fule in the van so non of the team players show up on time for the game.

The umpir is grompy.

The beutiful playing field is covered in mud.

You hear a crunh when you kick the ball.

You blash when you slip and fall.

You need a cruth to get off the field.

And finally, you don't get to play mutch.

_____   _____

_____   _____

_____   _____

_____   _____

_____   _____

_____   _____

Building Spelling Skills

WEEK 8

Spelling List

This Week's Focus:
- Spell words with double consonants
- Divide words with double consonants into syllables

STEP 1 Read and Spell

STEP 2 Copy and Spell

STEP 3 Cover and Spell

1. follow
2. matter
3. summer
4. million
5. dollar
6. scissors
7. cattle
8. address
9. office
10. suppertime
11. blizzard
12. penny
13. wrapper
14. wallet
15. occurrence
16. village
17. collide
18. battle
19. _____ bonus word
20. _____ bonus word

Building Spelling Skills, Daily Practice • EMC 6684   32   © Evan-Moor Corporation

Word Meaning

Complete the crossword puzzle using spelling words.

Down

1. a place of employment
3. the location of a building
4. to go behind
6. material
8. a large number
10. less than a nickel

Across

2. a small town
5. a happening
7. a season
9. 8 quarters = 2 _____
11. a container for money
12. an outer paper covering

My Spelling Dictation

Write the sentences. Circle the spelling words.

1. _____

2. _____

Word Study

Building Spelling Skills — WEEK 8

Fill in the missing double letters to make spelling words.

cc dd ff ll mm nn pp rr ss tt zz

1. a____ress
2. bli____ard
3. wa____et
4. co____ide
5. o____ice
6. wra____er
7. pe____y
8. mi____ion
9. vi____age
10. ba____le
11. fo____ow
12. sci____ors
13. ma____er
14. su____er
15. ca____le
16. do____ar
17. su____ertime
18. o____u____ence

Match syllables to make spelling words.
Write the complete words on the lines.

1. fol   lide   _____
2. bat   low   _____
3. mat   ter   _____
4. col   tle   _____
5. of   tle   _____
6. cat   fice   _____

7. vil   ny   _____
8. wal   lar   _____
9. pen   lage   _____
10. scis let   _____
11. dol   sors   _____
12. mil   lion   _____

Building Spelling Skills, Daily Practice • EMC 6684

Edit for Spelling

Building Spelling Skills

WEEK 8

Circle the words that are spelled correctly.

folow	dollar	walet	village
collide	batle	matler	cattle
rapper	peny	occurence	suppertime
million	adress	summer	scisors

Circle the misspelled words in the sentences.
Write them correctly on the lines.

1. My ofice is in a small villag.

   _____   _____

2. My addres is 402 Sumer Lane.

   _____   _____

3. I folow the rule to never run with scisors.

   _____   _____

4. Your change is four dollers and one pennie.

   _____   _____

5. The blizzerd must have had a millon snowflakes.

   _____   _____

6. Did you see the catle batle over that salt lick?

   _____   _____

© Evan-Moor Corporation   35   Building Spelling Skills, Daily Practice • EMC 6684

Building Spelling Skills

WEEK 9

Spelling List

This Week's Focus:
- Spell time and calendar words
- Identify word origins

STEP 1 Read and Spell

1. Tuesday
2. Wednesday
3. Thursday
4. Saturday
5. January
6. February
7. July
8. August
9. September
10. November
11. month
12. year
13. holiday
14. autumn
15. season
16. calendar
17. second
18. minute
19. _____ bonus word
20. _____ bonus word

STEP 2 Copy and Spell

STEP 3 Cover and Spell

Building Spelling Skills, Daily Practice • EMC 6684

© Evan-Moor Corporation

Word Meaning

Building Spelling Skills — WEEK 9

Answer these questions using spelling words.

1. Name the months.

   a. _____   d. _____

   b. _____   e. _____

   c. _____   f. _____

2. Name the days of the week.

   a. _____   c. _____

   b. _____   d. _____

3. What has 12 months in it?
   _____

4. What has about 30 days in it?
   _____

Fill in the blanks using spelling words.

1. Autumn is one of the four _____.

2. A _____ can be used to know the day and date.

My Spelling Dictation

Write the sentences. Circle the spelling words.

1. _____
   _____
   _____

2. _____
   _____
   _____

Word Study

Building Spelling Skills — WEEK 9

The days of the week are named for the sun, moon, and figures from mythology. Write the letter of the word origin on the line in front of the day.

_____ 1. Sunday   a. moon
_____ 2. Monday   b. Tiu, god of war
_____ 3. Tuesday   c. sun
_____ 4. Wednesday   d. Saturn, Roman god of farming
_____ 5. Thursday   e. Freya, Norse goddess of love
_____ 6. Friday   f. Thor, Norse god of thunder
_____ 7. Saturday   g. Woden, king of the Norse gods

The names of the months come from Latin, the language spoken in ancient Rome. Write the letter of the Latin word on the line in front of the month.

_____ 1. January   a. octo
_____ 2. February   b. decem
_____ 3. March   c. februa
_____ 4. April   d. septem
_____ 5. May   e. novem
_____ 6. June   f. Janus
_____ 7. July   g. aprilis
_____ 8. August   h. Maia
_____ 9. September   i. Mars
_____ 10. October   j. Juno
_____ 11. November   k. named after Augustus Caesar
_____ 12. December   l. named after Julius Caesar

Building Spelling Skills, Daily Practice • EMC 6684   © Evan-Moor Corporation

Edit for Spelling

Building Spelling Skills — WEEK 9

Circle the words that are spelled correctly.

September	seeson	calendr	holiday
year	month	Thursdey	Tuesday
atumn	Augest	July	Satureday
February	second	minate	Wednesday

Circle the misspelled words in the sentences.
Write them correctly on the lines.

1. Our holeday starts on Wednsday.

   _____ _____

2. Please find the mounth of Janary on the calendar.

   _____ _____

3. How many mintes and seconts did I take to run four laps?

   _____ _____

4. Tusday and Thersday are the days we have art class.

   _____ _____

5. Juli 4th is an important day in the United States.

   _____

6. I enjoy watching Satarday morning cartoons.

   _____

Building Spelling Skills

WEEK 10

Spelling List

This Week's Focus:
- Spell words with the schwa sound
- Spell words with the short **u** sound spelled **o**

STEP 1 Read and Spell

STEP 2 Copy and Spell

STEP 3 Cover and Spell

1. across
2. alone
3. among
4. brother
5. again
6. front
7. banana
8. appear
9. compass
10. pedal
11. given
12. heaven
13. mountain
14. ocean
15. cousin
16. purchase
17. often
18. color
19. _____ bonus word
20. _____ bonus word

Word Meaning

Building Spelling Skills — WEEK 10

Fill in the blanks with spelling words.

1. I went to the store to _____ a yellow _____.

2. I use a _____ to navigate my boat on the _____.

3. I had to _____ my bike _____ a bridge.

4. The climber reached the peak of the _____.

5. When my puppy is left _____, he starts to whine.

6. How _____ do you think the puppy will whine tonight?

7. I was _____ a red flower. That is my favorite _____.

8. Do you know my _____ and my _____?

9. Who will _____ when we knock on the _____ door?

10. I hope to see you _____ tomorrow.

My Spelling Dictation

Write the sentences. Circle the spelling words.

1. _____

2. _____

Word Study

Building Spelling Skills — WEEK 10

Write the symbol ə over the letter or letters that make the schwa sound.

ə			
across	alone	among	again
about	appear	brother	banana
compass	heaven	mountain	ocean
cousin	given	often	

Divide these words into syllables.

1. across   __a cross__
2. alone   _____
3. among   _____
4. again   _____
5. appear   _____
6. mountain   _____
7. brother   _____
8. compass   _____
9. banana   _____

10. given   _____
11. heaven   _____
12. ocean   _____
13. cousin   _____
14. purchase   _____
15. often   _____
16. color   _____
17. pedal   _____

Edit for Spelling

Building Spelling Skills — WEEK 10

Circle the word in each row that is spelled correctly.

1. heven   heaven   heavan   heavun
2. ocean   ocein   osean   oshun
3. collor   colar   coler   color
4. pedel   pedal   pedle   peddel
5. apear   apper   appere   appear
6. again   agin   agan   ugin
7. bananna   banana   banaana   bannana
8. frunt   frant   front   phrunt

Circle the misspelled words in the sentences.
Write them correctly on the lines.

1. My cousan, brothur, and I went on a hike acros the mowntens.

   _____   _____

   _____   _____

2. We pruchased a compas so we wouldn't get lost amung all the trees.

   _____   _____   _____   _____

3. It was awful to be all alon at night in the forest.

   _____

4. How ofton would you go on a hike if you were givan the chance?

   _____   _____

Building Spelling Skills

WEEK 11

Spelling List

This Week's Focus:
- Spell contractions

STEP 1 Read and Spell **STEP 2 Copy and Spell** **STEP 3 Cover and Spell**

1. didn't
2. that's
3. they're
4. you're
5. couldn't
6. haven't
7. o'clock
8. we're
9. isn't
10. I'm
11. it's
12. who's
13. they'd
14. could've
15. they've
16. you'll
17. don't
18. aren't
19. _____ bonus word
20. _____ bonus word

Word Meaning

Fill in the blanks with spelling words.

1. _____ all done with my homework.

2. I _____ want to do homework after 7 _____.

3. I wonder _____ knocking at the door?

4. Why _____ you playing outside?

5. It _____ my job to clean your room.

6. _____ anyone see what happened?

7. _____ time to go to school.

8. _____ going to our dance class.

9. _____ my best friend.

My Spelling Dictation

Write the sentences. Circle the spelling words.

1. _____

2. _____

Word Study

Building Spelling Skills

A contraction is a word formed from two words by leaving out some letters. Use an apostrophe to replace any missing letters.

Write the contraction. Then write the missing letter or letters.

1. are not   aren't   o
2. do not
3. you will
4. they have
5. could have
6. they would
7. who is
8. it is
9. I am
10. is not
11. we are
12. of the clock
13. have not
14. could not
15. you are
16. they are
17. that is
18. did not

Edit for Spelling

Building Spelling Skills

Write the missing apostrophe in the correct place.

1. Im
2. its
3. whos
4. theyd
5. couldve
6. theyve
7. youll
8. dont
9. arent
10. isnt
11. were
12. oclock
13. havent
14. couldnt
15. youre
16. thats
17. theyre
18. didnt

Circle the misspelled words in the sentences. Write them correctly on the lines.

1. Please doen't sit in that chair.

    _____

2. Thay're going to the store at 4 ol'clock.

    _____   _____

3. Who'se seen my cat? I doen't know where he's gone!

    _____   _____

4. You'r my best friend. Were' always having fun together.

    _____   _____

5. Thats what Im' going to do. You'l want to do it, too. Its fun.

    _____   _____

    _____   _____

Building Spelling Skills

WEEK 12

Spelling List

This Week's Focus:
- Spell compound words

STEP 1 Read and Spell

STEP 2 Copy and Spell

STEP 3 Cover and Spell

1. anyone
2. however
3. everything
4. himself
5. birthday
6. herself
7. somewhere
8. afternoon
9. chalkboard
10. daydream
11. downstairs
12. grandparents
13. breakfast
14. outfield
15. scarecrow
16. nobody
17. dragonfly
18. keyboard
19. _____ bonus word
20. _____ bonus word

Word Meaning

Complete the crossword puzzle using spelling words.

Down

1. in baseball, the area farthest from home plate
2. an early meal
3. a celebration
5. an insect
6. fantasy
7. where fingers go on computers

Across

4. the opposite of **herself**
8. one of your parents' parents
9. no one
10. any person
11. a figure made of straw

My Spelling Dictation

Write the sentences. Circle the spelling words.

1. _____

2. _____

Word Study

Building Spelling Skills — WEEK 12

A compound word is made from two shorter words.

Use one word from each column to make compound words. Cross out each word as you use it. Check your spelling to make sure that you form the compound words correctly.

Column 1	Column 2	Compound Words
chalk	parents	1. _____
some	noon	2. _____
after	ever	3. _____
how	self	4. _____
her	where	5. _____
grand	board	6. _____

Place a / between the parts of these compound words.

1. any/one
2. however
3. everything
4. himself
5. birthday
6. herself
7. somewhere
8. afternoon
9. chalkboard
10. daydream
11. downstairs
12. grandparents
13. breakfast
14. outfield
15. scarecrow
16. nobody
17. dragonfly
18. keyboard

Edit for Spelling

Circle the misspelled words in the sentences.
Write them correctly on the lines.

1. Will any one who is having a birth day please stand up?
   _____   _____

2. She wanted to do it her self. He wanted to do it hemself.
   _____   _____

3. This is every thing a dragon fly would eat.
   _____   _____

4. Somwhere on my key borad is the key I need.
   _____   _____

5. The teacher wrote the word "outfeild" on the chalk board.
   _____   _____

6. No body knew the name of the scarcrow.
   _____   _____

7. My grandparants always have break fast early in the morning.
   _____   _____

8. He was day dreaming down stairs in a soft chair.
   _____   _____

Circle the word in each row that is spelled correctly.

1. out field	outfield	out-field	outfeild
2. afternoon	after noon	after-noon	afternun
3. every-thing	every thing	evrything	everything
4. brakefast	breakfast	break fast	break-fast
5. no body	no-body	nobody	noobody

Building Spelling Skills

WEEK 13

Spelling List

This Week's Focus:
- Spell words with the endings -ing and -ed

Step 1: Read and Spell

1. lived
2. living
3. rattled
4. rattling
5. studied
6. studying
7. traveled
8. traveling
9. changed
10. changing
11. appeared
12. appearing
13. raced
14. racing
15. hoped
16. hoping
17. wrapped
18. wrapping
19. _____ bonus word
20. _____ bonus word

Step 2: Copy and Spell

Step 3: Cover and Spell

Word Meaning

Building Spelling Skills — WEEK 13

Complete these tasks using spelling words.

1. Write three verbs that are in the present tense.

   _____ _____ _____

2. Write three verbs that are in the past tense.

   _____ _____ _____

3. Write the base word that means...

   a. to go on a journey   _____

   b. to learn   _____

   c. to move quickly   _____

   d. to switch or alter   _____

   e. to exist   _____

   f. to wish   _____

   g. to clatter   _____

   h. to show up   _____

My Spelling Dictation

Write the sentences. Circle the spelling words.

1. _____

   _____

2. _____

   _____

Word Study

Building Spelling Skills — WEEK 13

Add **ing** to the base words. Write the new word on the line.
Check the box that shows how you changed the word.

	no change	drop e	double final consonant
1. live — living		✔	
2. wrap			
3. rattle			
4. hope			
5. study			
6. race			
7. travel			
8. change			
9. appear			

Add **ed** to the base words. Write the new word on the line.
Check the box that shows how you changed the word.

	no change	change y to i	drop e	double final consonant
1. live				
2. wrap				
3. rattle				
4. hope				
5. study				
6. race				
7. travel				
8. change				
9. appear				

Edit for Spelling

Circle the word in each row that is spelled correctly.

1. rattling   ratling   ratteling   rattlling
2. raceing   racing   rasing   rassing
3. travelled   travvled   travled   traveled
4. chanjing   changeing   changing   changeng
5. apearing   appearing   appearring   appering

Circle the 8 misspelled words below.
Write the words correctly on the lines.

Changing Appearances

Ian was travel down a dirt road. He race to one side of the road and saw a tiny object hanging from a tree branch. He study the object for a long time. After a while, it changd. The wraping around the object split open. Perhaps, Ian thought, something live inside and wanted out. Right before Ian's eyes appear a butterfly. It was beautiful! Ian hope he would see the butterfly again someday.

_____ _____

_____ _____

_____ _____

_____ _____

Building Spelling Skills

WEEK 14

Spelling List

This Week's Focus:
- Spell words with the endings -er and -est

Step 1: Read and Spell
Step 2: Copy and Spell
Step 3: Cover and Spell

1. cleaner
2. cleanest
3. bigger
4. biggest
5. earlier
6. earliest
7. quicker
8. quickest
9. busier
10. busiest
11. rougher
12. roughest
13. heavier
14. heaviest
15. happier
16. happiest
17. lazier
18. laziest
19. _____ bonus word
20. _____ bonus word

Word Meaning

Building Spelling Skills — WEEK 14

Complete the crossword puzzle using spelling words.

Down

1. less active than another person
2. doing more than anyone
3. larger than another thing
5. less smooth
7. more spotless
8. arriving before another person

Across

4. larger than anything
6. the opposite of **smoothest**
7. the most spotless
9. arriving before anyone
10. more weighty

My Spelling Dictation

Write the sentences. Circle the spelling words.

1. _____
   _____
   _____

2. _____
   _____
   _____

Word Study

Building Spelling Skills — WEEK 14

Add **er** to the base words. Write the new word on the line.
Check the box that shows how you changed the word.

	no change	change **y** to **i**	double final consonant
1. clean _____			
2. big _____			
3. early _____			
4. quick _____			
5. busy _____			
6. rough _____			
7. heavy _____			
8. happy _____			
9. lazy _____			

Add **est** to the base words. Write the new word on the line.
Check the box that shows how you changed the word.

	no change	change **y** to **i**	double final consonant
1. clean _____			
2. big _____			
3. early _____			
4. quick _____			
5. busy _____			
6. rough _____			
7. heavy _____			
8. happy _____			
9. lazy _____			

Building Spelling Skills, Daily Practice • EMC 6684 © Evan-Moor Corporation

Edit for Spelling

Building Spelling Skills — WEEK 14

Circle the words that are spelled correctly.

earlyest	busy	biggiest	quick
heaviest	besiest	biggier	quicker
lazy	buser	cleanest	happyest
lazyest	roughest	cleanier	happiest

Circle the incorrect word in each sentence.
Write it correctly on the line.

1. My dog is biggest than your dog. _____

2. I'm the earlest person here. _____

3. This is the lazier turtle in the zoo. _____

4. Who is happyer, Angela or Elizabeth? _____

5. My rock is heaviest than your rock. _____

6. I'm busyest in the summer. _____

7. Which way is the quickiest? _____

8. You have the cleaniest room in the house! _____

9. This wood feels roughor than that wood. _____

10. You seem to be the hapiest person here. _____

11. The teacher looks busyer than the students. _____

Building Spelling Skills

WEEK 15

Spelling List

This Week's Focus:
- Spell words with the /ur/ sound spelled **er**, **ir**, **ur**, **ear**, **or**, and **ar**

STEP 1 Read and Spell

1. early
2. earth
3. search
4. service
5. wonder
6. surface
7. curly
8. shirt
9. thirty
10. doctor
11. sailor
12. shower
13. bakery
14. another
15. barber
16. collar
17. worse
18. world
19. _____ bonus word
20. _____ bonus word

STEP 2 Copy and Spell

STEP 3 Cover and Spell

Word Meaning

Building Spelling Skills — WEEK 15

Fill in the blanks with spelling words.

1. Before you wash your _____, rub soap on the _____.

2. There's nothing _____ in this _____ than wobbly skates.

3. The _____ told the _____ he was seasick.

4. The _____ cut off all the boy's _____ hair.

5. The dry _____ welcomes the rain _____.

6. With such bad _____, it is a _____ how this _____ stays in business.

7. The _____ bird usually gets the worm, but this time _____ bird got it.

8. Can a submarine dive _____ miles below the _____ of the ocean?

My Spelling Dictation

Write the sentences. Circle the spelling words.

1. _____
   _____
   _____

2. _____
   _____
   _____

Word Study

Building Spelling Skills — WEEK 15

Fill in the missing letters to make spelling words.

> or   er   ar   ur   ir

1. doct_____
2. barb_____
3. show_____
4. wond_____
5. sail_____
6. anoth_____
7. coll_____

8. s_____vice
9. w_____se
10. bak_____y
11. w_____ld
12. th_____ty
13. c_____ly
14. sh_____t

Divide these words into syllables. Check your answers in a dictionary.

1. early _____ _____
2. thirty _____ _____
3. doctor _____ _____
4. service _____ _____
5. wonder _____ _____
6. barber _____ _____
7. surface _____ _____
8. curly _____ _____
9. sailor _____ _____
10. shower _____ _____
11. collar _____ _____

Building Spelling Skills, Daily Practice • EMC 6684   62   © Evan-Moor Corporation

Edit for Spelling

Circle the 12 misspelled words below.
Write them correctly on the lines.

Building Spelling Skills — WEEK 15

Earth Day Excitement

Ms. Spring brought her class of therty students to an Erth Day workshop. They learned many things about caring for our wurld.

1. A rain showor can wash away the top serface of soil that doesn't have plants growing in it.

2. The survice of a tree docter may be needed to save a sick tree.

3. There's nothing much wors you can do than pollute groundwater.

Ms. Spring's class stayed at the workshop until erly evening. When it was time to go, everyone had to sarch for a missing student. It didn't take long to find her because her bright white sailer suit and cerly red hair stood out in the crowd.

_____   _____

_____   _____

_____   _____

_____   _____

_____   _____

_____   _____

Building Spelling Skills

WEEK 16

Spelling List

This Week's Focus:
- Spell singular and plural forms of words

STEP 1 Read and Spell
STEP 2 Copy and Spell
STEP 3 Cover and Spell

1. leaf
2. leaves
3. wolf
4. wolves
5. potato
6. potatoes
7. roof
8. roofs
9. family
10. families
11. library
12. libraries
13. journey
14. journeys
15. hero
16. heroes
17. ditch
18. ditches
19. _____ bonus word
20. _____ bonus word

Word Meaning

Complete the crossword puzzle using spelling words.

Down
1. several trips
2. a single plant part
3. an admired person
6. parts of plants
7. more than one trench
8. a trench
9. many house coverings
12. a root vegetable

Across
4. several wild canines
5. a single trip
10. several groups of relatives
11. a wild canine
13. persons of great courage
14. more than two root vegetables
15. a house covering

My Spelling Dictation

Write the sentences. Circle the spelling words.

1. _____

2. _____

Word Study

Building Spelling Skills — WEEK 16

Change each singular noun to its plural form.
Check the box that shows how you changed the word.

	add **s** or **es**	change **y** to **i** add **es**	change **f** to **v** add **es**
1. leaf _____			
2. hero _____			
3. potato _____			
4. family _____			
5. ditch _____			
6. wolf _____			
7. library _____			
8. journey _____			

Divide these words into syllables.

1. heroes _____ _____

2. ditches _____ _____

3. journeys _____ _____

4. potatoes _____ _____ _____

5. families _____ _____ _____

6. libraries _____ _____ _____

Building Spelling Skills, Daily Practice • EMC 6684 © Evan-Moor Corporation

Edit for Spelling

Building Spelling Skills

WEEK 16

Circle the words that are spelled correctly.

famíles	libraries	leafs
heros	potatoes	ditches
journeyes	roofes	wolves

Circle the misspelled words in the sentences.
Write them correctly on the lines.

1. My famile looks for aluminum cans in ditchs.
   _____   _____

2. The herow of the story ate potatos.
   _____   _____

3. There were a lot of leafs on the rooves.
   _____   _____

4. The wolfs went on a long journy.
   _____   _____

5. All the familes in my neighborhood like to go to the librare.
   _____   _____

6. He made one last effort to keep the rouf from catching fire.
   _____

7. My dog, who is part woolf, is over there chasing a leef.
   _____   _____

8. Books about heros can be found in all libraryes.
   _____   _____

Building Spelling Skills

WEEK 17

Spelling List

This Week's Focus:
- Spell words with the /aw/ sound spelled **al**, **ough**, **o**, **au**, and **aw**

STEP 1 Read and Spell

1. also
2. bought
3. cough
4. almost
5. false
6. officer
7. soft
8. stalk
9. halt
10. faucet
11. saucer
12. caution
13. lawyer
14. awesome
15. stall
16. crawl
17. awful
18. because
19. _____ bonus word
20. _____ bonus word

STEP 2 Copy and Spell

STEP 3 Cover and Spell

Word Meaning

Building Spelling Skills

Answer the questions using spelling words.

1. Which spelling word is a synonym for…?

    a. too _____

    b. creep _____

    c. untrue _____

    d. gentle _____

2. Which spelling word is an antonym for…?

    a. hard _____

    b. go _____

    c. true _____

    d. sold _____

3. Which spelling word means…?

    a. a person who enforces the law
    _____

    b. a plumbing fixture
    _____

    c. a cup's partner
    _____

    d. a person who studies the law
    _____

    e. to expel air noisily
    _____

    f. for the reason that
    _____

    g. in addition
    _____

    h. to move on all fours
    _____

My Spelling Dictation

Write the sentences. Circle the spelling words.

1. _____
   _____
   _____

2. _____
   _____
   _____

Word Study

Building Spelling Skills — WEEK 17

Write the spelling words in the correct boxes.

also	bought	cough	almost	false	officer
soft	stalk	halt	faucet	saucer	caution
lawyer	awesome	stall	crawl	awful	because

a as in fall	au as in caught	aw as in law	o as in loft	ou as in trough

Match syllables to make words.
Write the complete words on the lines.

1. be — some   1. _____
2. awe — cause   2. _____
3. al — cet   3. _____
4. law — so   4. _____
5. fau — yer   5. _____
6. sau — tion   6. _____
7. cau — most   7. _____
8. al — cer   8. _____

Building Spelling Skills, Daily Practice • EMC 6684 © Evan-Moor Corporation

Edit for Spelling

Building Spelling Skills

Circle the words that are spelled correctly.

cation	almost	cough	allso
lawyer	oficer	faucet	stalk
fallse	bought	stall	crall
awful	becaus	awesome	saucer

Circle the misspelled words in the sentences.
Write them correctly on the lines.

1. She all most dropped the sawcer.
   _____   _____

2. The layer took great cawtion with the case.
   _____   _____

3. It was awsome to see the baby crall.
   _____   _____

4. He baht a saft blanket.
   _____   _____

5. It was auful to hear him cauf.
   _____   _____

6. The kitchen faucat was dripping becauze it was old.
   _____   _____

7. The offisor yelled, "Hallt!"
   _____   _____

8. That's allso a fallse statement.
   _____   _____

Building Spelling Skills

WEEK 18

Spelling List

This Week's Focus:
- Spell words with the variant sounds of **c** and **g**

STEP 1 Read and Spell

STEP 2 Copy and Spell

STEP 3 Cover and Spell

1. cinder
2. circle
3. cardinal
4. cereal
5. cycle
6. concert
7. dancer
8. celebrate
9. twice
10. dangerous
11. strange
12. ledge
13. damage
14. geography
15. gentle
16. signal
17. regular
18. sugar
19. _____ bonus word
20. _____ bonus word

Word Meaning

Fill in the blanks in the paragraphs below with spelling words.

The Day the Dancer Fell

I have been a _____ for many years. A _____ and _____ situation happened to me one night while I was performing. I was dancing in a large _____ when a _____ flew past my head. I was frightened, and stepped too close to the edge of the stage. I fell into the orchestra pit. Luckily, I had a _____ landing. I fell right on a gigantic bass drum! There was no _____ to me or the drum.

Getting Ready to Sing

Every morning I eat a bowl of _____ with two spoonfuls of _____. I try to put more on, but my dad always gives a _____ to stop. After breakfast my _____ routine is to get dressed for school. This morning, however, I must put on my best dress. I want to look nice when I sing in our school choir _____.

My Spelling Dictation

Write the sentences. Circle the spelling words.

1. _____

_____

2. _____

_____

Word Study

Building Spelling Skills — WEEK 18

Write the spelling words in the correct boxes.

soft c sound as in face	hard c sound as in cat	soft g sound as in giant	hard g sound as in great

Write the spelling words that mean about the same as these words.

1. a repeating event _____
2. round _____
3. to honor _____
4. study of the earth _____
5. gesture _____
6. calm _____
7. odd _____
8. harmful _____

Write the spelling words that mean the opposite of these words.

1. repair _____
2. safe _____
3. usual _____
4. harsh _____

Edit for Spelling

Building Spelling Skills — WEEK 18

Circle the words that are spelled correctly.

strange	sereal	consert
cinder	ledge	sugar
gentel	twise	cycle
cardinal	danser	geographe
regular	damege	dangerous

Circle the misspelled words in the sentences.
Write them correctly on the lines.

1. The dansir leapt twise.

   _____   _____

2. The cardinel ate cerial from my bowl.

   _____   _____

3. It is dangerus to sit on the lege.

   _____   _____

4. The geograpy of the desert was strang.

   _____   _____

5. We used reguler sinder blocks to make the house.

   _____   _____

6. There was a lot of damege to the signel light.

   _____   _____

Building Spelling Skills

WEEK 19

Spelling List

This Week's Focus:
- Spell words with the /oo/ sound spelled **ew, o, oe, oo, ou, ough, u, ue,** and **ui**

Step 1 Read and Spell

1. shoes
2. clues
3. wound
4. junior
5. truth
6. duty
7. news
8. through
9. few
10. who
11. schoolroom
12. whose
13. conclusion
14. June
15. shampoo
16. cruel
17. choose
18. ruin
19. _____ bonus word
20. _____ bonus word

Step 2 Copy and Spell

Step 3 Cover and Spell

Word Meaning

Building Spelling Skills — WEEK 19

Complete the crossword puzzle using spelling words.

Down
1. hints
2. the opposite of **many**
5. to destroy
7. word used when asking about ownership
8. a month
9. to select
11. to hurt

Across
3. responsibility
4. mean
6. information
9. an ending
10. footwear
11. which person?
12. a place to learn

My Spelling Dictation

Write the sentences. Circle the spelling words.

1. _____

2. _____

Word Study

Building Spelling Skills — WEEK 19

Fill in the missing letters to make spelling words.

> ew   o   oe   oo   ou   ough   u   ue   ui

1. f_____
2. sch_____lroom
3. J_____ne
4. cr_____l
5. sh_____s
6. tr_____th
7. d_____ty
8. wh_____
9. ch_____se
10. r_____in
11. thr_____
12. n_____s
13. wh_____se
14. concl_____sion
15. shamp_____
16. w_____nd
17. cl_____s
18. j_____nior

Read each word. Write the number of syllables on the line.

1. shoes _____
2. clues _____
3. wound _____
4. junior _____
5. truth _____
6. duty _____
7. news _____
8. through _____
9. few _____
10. who _____
11. schoolroom _____
12. whose _____
13. conclusion _____
14. June _____
15. shampoo _____
16. cruel _____
17. choose _____
18. ruin _____

Edit for Spelling

Circle the 14 misspelled words below.
Write the words correctly on the lines.

The Big Bell Caper

Mr. Dell's bell was missing from his schoolrom. He used the bell during recess dooty. He would ring his bell to let students know when to return to class. Nuws of the missing bell traveled quickly thrugh the school.

There were feu cloos. Mr. Dell came to the conclosion that he would never see his bell again. The troth was, he was woonded. Whu would be so crul as to take his bell? His students said they would become juinor detectives and help him find his bell before june.

Then a familiar ringing was heard. Ms. Nell, whos room is next-door, must have forgotten to tell Mr. Dell that she borrowed his swell bell.

Building Spelling Skills

WEEK 20

Spelling List

This Week's Focus:
- Spell words with the /oi/ sound spelled **oi** and **oy**
- Spell words with the /ow/ sound spelled **ow** and **ou**

STEP 1 Read and Spell

STEP 2 Copy and Spell

STEP 3 Cover and Spell

1. voice
2. oyster
3. voyage
4. annoy
5. choice
6. avoid
7. appoint
8. enjoy
9. moisture
10. noise
11. drown
12. amount
13. fountain
14. crowded
15. southwest
16. thousand
17. flour
18. pronounce
19. _____ bonus word
20. _____ bonus word

Word Meaning

Fill in the blanks with spelling words.

The Meeting

I went to our student council meeting. The room was so _____, few students had a place to sit. No one could hear what was going on. The president's _____ was too quiet, and there was lots of _____ in the room. She had to _____ a sergeant-at-arms to bring order to the meeting. This helped a lot. Everyone quieted down in a short _____ of time. After that, the meeting was successful.

The Voyage

Kawa went on an ocean _____ a _____ miles long. Most of the trip was in the _____ern part of the Pacific Ocean. And try as she might, she could never learn to _____ the ship's name. While on the trip, she ate an _____. She especially liked it dipped in _____ and fried. If she were given the _____, she would eat them all day long. She will _____ memories of her trip forever.

My Spelling Dictation

Write the sentences. Circle the spelling words.

1. _____
_____
_____

2. _____
_____
_____

Word Study

Building Spelling Skills — WEEK 20

Circle the letters that make the vowel sound in **boy**.

1. v(oi)ce
2. oyster
3. voyage
4. annoy
5. choice
6. avoid
7. appoint
8. enjoy
9. moisture
10. noise

Circle the letters that make the vowel sound in **cow**.

1. drown
2. amount
3. fountain
4. crowded
5. southwest
6. thousand
7. flour
8. pronounce

Match syllables to make spelling words.
Write the complete words on the lines.

1. oys	nounce	1. _____
2. an	ter	2. _____
3. pro	tain	3. _____
4. foun	noy	4. _____
5. a	mount	5. _____
6. thou	ture	6. _____
7. south	sand	7. _____
8. mois	west	8. _____
9. en	age	9. _____
10. voy	joy	10. _____

Building Spelling Skills, Daily Practice • EMC 6684
© Evan-Moor Corporation

Edit for Spelling

Building Spelling Skills — WEEK 20

Circle the word in each row that is spelled correctly.

1. amownt — amount — amunt — umont
2. thousand — thousant — thowsand — thosand
3. injoy — enjoe — enjoi — enjoy
4. voeage — voyage — vowage — voiage
5. voic — voece — voise — voice
6. apoint — appont — appoint — apont
7. pronounce — pronownce — prononce — pronunce
8. sowthwest — southwest — sothwest — south west

Circle the misspelled words in the sentences.
Write them correctly on the lines.

1. Please don't anoy the cat with noice.
   _____   _____

2. Try to avoed putting too much water on the plant. It will droun.
   _____   _____

3. My choece is to eat the oister.
   _____   _____

4. The bag of flowr spilled all over the floor.
   _____

5. The elevator was too crouded.
   _____

6. The weather was so humid that moistur dripped from my glass.
   _____

Building Spelling Skills

WEEK 21

Spelling List

This Week's Focus:
- Spell words with the /f/ sound spelled **f**, **ff**, **ph**, and **gh**

STEP 1 Read and Spell

STEP 2 Copy and Spell

STEP 3 Cover and Spell

1. enough
2. tougher
3. fifty
4. pharmacy
5. alphabet
6. nephew
7. trophy
8. paragraph
9. telephone
10. photograph
11. giraffe
12. forest
13. figure
14. refrigerator
15. draft
16. phrase
17. traffic
18. chief
19. _____ bonus word
20. _____ bonus word

Word Meaning

Complete the crossword puzzle using spelling words.

Across
1. a group of words
2. a sufficient amount
4. a leader
7. a section of a piece of writing
10. a drugstore
11. a communication device

Down
1. a picture
3. a relative
5. the number after forty, by tens
6. an award
8. 26 letters
9. a first writing effort

My Spelling Dictation

Write the sentences. Circle the spelling words.

1. _____

2. _____

Word Study

Building Spelling Skills — WEEK 21

Circle the letters that make the /f/ sound.

1. enou(gh)
2. tougher
3. fifty
4. pharmacy
5. alphabet
6. nephew
7. trophy
8. paragraph
9. telephone
10. photograph
11. giraffe
12. forest
13. figure
14. refrigerator
15. draft
16. phrase
17. traffic
18. chief

Fill in the missing letters. Write **f**, **ff**, **gh**, or **ph**.

1. ___f___igure
2. gira_____e
3. _____i_____ty
4. tra_____ic
5. dra_____t
6. al_____abet
7. paragra_____
8. tro_____y
9. chie_____
10. _____rase
11. re_____rigerator
12. _____armacy
13. enou_____
14. _____orest
15. _____otogra_____
16. tele_____one
17. ne_____ew
18. tou_____er

Edit for Spelling

Circle the 12 misspelled words below.
Write the words correctly on the lines.

The Fifty-Float Chief

The race was on at the soda fountain in Phil's Farmacy. My nehew was trying to make fity root beer floats in less than 15 minutes. The task was toufer than he thought. He figured he had just enouf time to make the final few floats.

There was a fourest of glasses on the counter. People had to stretch their necks like girafes to see the final scoop of ice cream plop into the glass. The splash in the glass was heard just before the buzzer sounded.

My nefew was presented a terrific trophe. The next morning's newspaper had a photograf and a well-written pargraph about his feat. He was named the cheif of root beer floats!

Building Spelling Skills

WEEK 22

Spelling List

This Week's Focus:
- Spell words with **ight**, **ought**, **aught**, and **au**

STEP 1 Read and Spell

1. frighten
2. flight
3. brighter
4. flashlight
5. mighty
6. delight
7. tighten
8. nightly
9. sight
10. brought
11. ought
12. thought
13. fought
14. caught
15. daughter
16. taught
17. naughty
18. fault
19. _____ bonus word
20. _____ bonus word

STEP 2 Copy and Spell

STEP 3 Cover and Spell

Word Meaning

Fill in the blanks with spelling words.
Two of the spelling words are used twice in the story.

The Nightly Fright

A few night ago, my young _____ _____ she heard a noise coming from our basement. The same thing happened the next evening. She _____ me to the basement door more than once, but I never heard a thing. This _____ event, however, continued to _____ her. One night I decided to go down the _____ of stairs to see for myself. I shined my _____ from one corner of the basement to another. Finally, my light _____ _____ of a pair of yellowish dots that became _____ and _____. To my _____, it was just our _____ kitty playing in a box of yarn. Now my _____ always makes sure the basement door is closed.

My Spelling Dictation

Write the sentences. Circle the spelling words.

1. _____

_____

_____

2. _____

_____

_____

Word Study

Building Spelling Skills — WEEK 22

Add the correct letters to make words.

> ight   ought   aught

1. fl_____   4. c_____

2. del_____   5. br_____

3. th_____   6. br_____

Circle the letters that make the sound of **a** in **father**.

1. brought   5. caught
2. fault   6. daughter
3. thought   7. taught
4. fought   8. naughty

Circle the letters that make the sound of **i** in **pie**.

1. frighten   5. mighty
2. flight   6. delight
3. brighter   7. tighten
4. flashlight   8. nightly

All the spelling words except one have a pair of silent letters. What are those letters?

_____ _____

Edit for Spelling

Building Spelling Skills — WEEK 22

Circle the words that are spelled correctly.

caught	dauhter	thaught	delight
brightor	taught	faught	ought
sight	brihter	frightan	tought

Circle the misspelled words in the sentences.
Write them correctly on the lines.

1. I aught to tighton the lid.

   _____ _____

2. It was my fallt that we fouht.

   _____ _____

3. I cought a flit to Denver.

   _____ _____

4. My daughtor taght her dog to sit up.

   _____ _____

5. He used the flashlite nitly.

   _____ _____

6. That sieght would frihten anyone.

   _____ _____

7. I thougt that child was very naghty.

   _____ _____

8. His funny joke broght deliht to the crowd.

   _____ _____

9. That toothpaste helped me have a brihter smile.

   _____

Building Spelling Skills

WEEK 23

Spelling List

This Week's Focus:
- Spell words with silent letters

STEP 1 Read and Spell

STEP 2 Copy and Spell

STEP 3 Cover and Spell

1. calf
2. walked
3. ghost
4. gnawed
5. climber
6. wreath
7. listen
8. island
9. scent
10. wrench
11. judge
12. fasten
13. wrist
14. doubt
15. knock
16. answer
17. knelt
18. sign
19. _____ bonus word
20. _____ bonus word

Word Meaning

Complete the crossword puzzle using spelling words.
There are three words that are not on your spelling list. Try to figure them out.

Building Spelling Skills

WEEK 23

Down
1. went onto your knees
2. to secure
3. the reply to a question
4. a circular decoration
5. a baby cow
6. land with water all around it
10. a person who goes up a mountain
11. an object used to unlock a door
12. a body part below the mouth
14. someone who decides cases

Across
4. a tool
7. a smell
8. to hear
9. to taste food
11. to tap on a door
13. strolled
15. a symbol
16. to be unsure
17. the joint above the hand

My Spelling Dictation

Write the sentences. Circle the spelling words.

1. _____

2. _____

© Evan-Moor Corporation
Building Spelling Skills, Daily Practice • EMC 6684

Word Study

Building Spelling Skills — WEEK 23

Circle the letters that are silent.

1. ca(l)f
2. walked
3. ghost
4. gnawed
5. climber
6. wreath
7. listen
8. island
9. scent
10. wrench
11. judge
12. fasten
13. wrist
14. doubt
15. knock
16. answer
17. knelt
18. sign

Fill in the missing letters to make spelling words.

> d   b   c   g   k   l   t   w

1. ____nelt
2. ____nock
3. ____rist
4. ____rench
5. ____reath
6. ____nawed
7. si____n
8. ca____f
9. wa____ked
10. clim____er
11. lis____en
12. fas____en
13. ans____er
14. dou____t
15. ju____ge
16. s____ent

Write the spelling words that mean about the same as these words.

1. strolled _____
2. close _____
3. spirit _____
4. chewed _____
5. hear _____
6. reply _____

Edit for Spelling

Building Spelling Skills

Correct the spelling of these words.

1. wrinch _____
2. wreeth _____
3. walkt _____
4. gnawd _____
5. knok _____

6. answor _____
7. dowt _____
8. wrest _____
9. judg _____
10. climbor _____

Circle the misspelled words in the sentences. Write them correctly on the lines.

1. Lisson! Was that a nock at the door?

   _____   _____

2. The caf nelt down to get a drink of water.

   _____   _____

3. I dout that we need a stop sing here.

   _____   _____

4. Did the juge give you an anser?

   _____   _____

5. Did the climer fason the rope correctly?

   _____   _____

6. The iland had the pleasant cent of flowers.

   _____   _____

7. He looked at the watch on his wist before he waked to the store.

   _____   _____

8. She needed to use a rench to put up the large reath.

   _____   _____

Building Spelling Skills

WEEK 24

Spelling List

This Week's Focus:
- Add the suffixes **-ion**, **-tion**, **-sion**, and **-cian** to base words and word roots

STEP 1 Read and Spell
STEP 2 Copy and Spell
STEP 3 Cover and Spell

1. action
2. fiction
3. mission
4. divide
5. division
6. attend
7. attention
8. pollute
9. pollution
10. express
11. expression
12. educate
13. education
14. music
15. musician
16. magic
17. magician
18. physician
19. _____ bonus word
20. _____ bonus word

Word Meaning

Use spelling words to answer the clues.

1. a person who takes care of our physical health _____
2. a person who performs magic _____
3. a person who creates music _____
4. to learn something you must give it this _____
5. teachers want their students to get this _____
6. environmentalists worry about this _____
7. an operation with numbers _____
8. stories that are made up by the author _____
9. an exciting story has lots of this _____
10. something you should use when you read aloud _____

Which spelling word is an antonym for…?

1. clean _____
2. multiply _____
3. fact _____
4. inaction _____

My Spelling Dictation

Write the sentences. Circle the spelling words.

1. _____

2. _____

Building Spelling Skills WEEK 24

Word Study

Building Spelling Skills — WEEK 24

Add the correct suffix to the base word.
You may need to make a change to the base word before adding the suffix.

> ion   tion   sion

1. An _____ I like is, "It's raining cats and dogs."
   express

2. There is a lot of _____ on the football field.
   act

3. I need your _____.
   attend

4. I enjoy learning about _____ in math class.
   divide

5. My _____ is very important to me.
   educate

6. There is _____ in the river.
   pollute

Write each word from the spelling list in the correct box.

two-syllable words	three-syllable words	four-syllable words

Building Spelling Skills, Daily Practice • EMC 6684   98   © Evan-Moor Corporation

Edit for Spelling

Building Spelling Skills — WEEK 24

Circle the 20 misspelled words below. Three words are misspelled more than once. Write the words correctly on the lines.

On a Mission

A musicion, a magicion, and a physicion went on a hike in the mountains. The musican said the mountains brought musik to her heart. The magician's expression was that the mountains were magical. The phsician, however, said the mountains reminded her of sprained ankles.

The muician liked to focus her atention on listening to the songs of the birds. The magikian would always xpres her amazement at how fast chipmunks could disappear. The fasician, however, looked for twigs that could be used for splints.

The musician enjoyed being in a place where there was no sound polution. The magecian enjoyed watching beavers divid tree branches in half. The phasician, however, worried about whether she brought enough poison ivy lotion.

Toward the end of the hike, it became the mision of the musecian and mugician to help the physcan "doctor" her attitude so she could enjoy the remainder of the day.

_____   _____
_____   _____
_____   _____
_____   _____
_____   _____
_____   _____
_____   _____
_____   _____
_____   _____
_____   _____

Building Spelling Skills

WEEK 25

Spelling List

This Week's Focus:
- Spell two- and three-syllable words
- Identify beginning open syllables

STEP 1 Read and Spell | **STEP 2 Copy and Spell** | **STEP 3 Cover and Spell**

1. lazy
2. volcano
3. flavor
4. piano
5. recent
6. really
7. item
8. pilot
9. triangle
10. climate
11. gigantic
12. program
13. obey
14. puny
15. prepare
16. vacant
17. pulley
18. menu
19. _____ bonus word
20. _____ bonus word

Word Meaning

Building Spelling Skills — WEEK 25

Fill in the blanks with spelling words.

1. The _____ flew his plane close to the erupting _____.

2. The _____ was so hot and humid that everyone felt _____ and didn't want to work.

3. He played an amazing song on the _____ during the _____.

4. My favorite _____ of ice cream on the _____ is strawberry.

5. They needed a _____ _____ to lift the car.

6. I must _____ dinner for the guests.

7. A _____ study said that juice is _____ good for you.

8. The _____ little dog would always _____ his master.

9. No one lives in the _____ building shaped like a _____.

My Spelling Dictation

Write the sentences. Circle the spelling words.

1. _____

_____

2. _____

_____

Word Study

Building Spelling Skills — WEEK 25

An open syllable ends with a long vowel sound.
Underline the words that begin with an open syllable.
Circle the beginning open syllable in each word you underline.

1. (la)zy
2. volcano
3. flavor
4. piano
5. recent
6. menu
7. pilot
8. triangle
9. climate
10. gigantic
11. pulley
12. program
13. obey
14. puny
15. prepare
16. vacant

Fill in the missing letters to make spelling words.

la_____   _____tem   real_____   _____gantic

fla_____   _____bey   pi_____o   tri_____gle

Match a first and second syllable to create spelling words.
Write them on the lines.

First	
la	cli
re	o
men	i

Second	
tem	bey
zy	mate
u	cent

_____   _____

_____   _____

_____   _____

Edit for Spelling

Building Spelling Skills — WEEK 25

Circle the words that are spelled correctly.

climate	giganic	triangal	peano
recent	itum	pilot	puny
vakent	obey	program	realy
laze	volcano	flaver	pully

Circle the misspelled words in the sentences. Write them correctly on the lines.

1. The lawyer was so lasy that he had a vakint office.
   _____   _____

2. Did you see the itam in the newspaper about the valcano?
   _____   _____

3. Which is your favorite flaver, Gigantac Grape or Large Lime?
   _____   _____

4. The pielot realle wants his own plane.
   _____   _____

5. We are pleased with our resent pieno purchase.
   _____   _____

6. Please oby the rules when using that puley.
   _____   _____

7. There's not much on that punee menue.
   _____   _____

8. The climat in the Bermuda Triangel was warm.
   _____   _____

9. He will pripar snacks before watching the TV programe.
   _____   _____

Building Spelling Skills

WEEK 26

Spelling List

This Week's Focus:
- Spell homophones

STEP 1 Read and Spell

STEP 2 Copy and Spell

STEP 3 Cover and Spell

1. herd
2. heard
3. clothes
4. close
5. hour
6. our
7. two
8. too
9. their
10. there
11. ceiling
12. sealing
13. shoot
14. chute
15. strait
16. straight
17. medal
18. meddle
19. _____ bonus word
20. _____ bonus word

Word Meaning

Complete the crossword puzzle using spelling words.

Down

1. also
3. belonging to them
4. a steep slide; a tight space
5. closing tightly
7. an award
8. listened
9. the opposite of **open**
11. belonging to us
12. the number after **one**

Across

2. a sprout
5. the opposite of **curved**
6. a narrow strip of water
8. a group of cows
9. the top of a room
10. 60 minutes
12. in that place

My Spelling Dictation

Write the sentences. Circle the spelling words.

1. _____

2. _____

Word Study

Building Spelling Skills — WEEK 26

Write the spelling words that are homophones for these words.

1. heard _____
2. clothes _____
3. hour _____
4. medal _____
5. strait _____
6. chute _____
7. sealing _____
8. two _____
9. their _____

Choose the correct words to fill in the blanks.

1. I want to go over _____. That box contains _____ toys.
   (their, there)   (their, there)

2. Please be back in one _____. This is _____ house.
   (hour, our)   (hour, our)

3. Let's _____ some hoops. Is the bull in its _____?
   (chute, shoot)   (chute, shoot)

4. I have _____ dogs. She has a dog, _____.
   (two, too)   (two, too)

5. Our boat is in the _____. We're moving _____ ahead.
   (strait, straight)   (strait, straight)

6. Please don't _____ in my problems. He won a _____.
   (meddle, medal)   (meddle, medal)

7. Did you paint the _____? Are you _____ the paint can?
   (sealing, ceiling)   (sealing, ceiling)

8. Do you like _____ clock? One _____ has passed already.
   (our, hour)   (our, hour)

9. Please _____ the closet door. Then put on your _____.
   (close, clothes)   (close, clothes)

Building Spelling Skills, Daily Practice • EMC 6684 — © Evan-Moor Corporation

Edit for Spelling

Circle the 14 misspelled words below.
Write the words correctly on the lines.

Building Spelling Skills — WEEK 26

The Dangerous Marble

I'm the marble champion of owr school. Their is no one better. I became a champion because I practice for an our every day. I can shot all the marbles out of a circle in less than too minutes.

During one game, a single "cat's-eye" was left in the circle. My shooter headed straht for it. The impact was so loud that everyone herd it. The marble bounced off the seiling and came way two clos to hitting a group of students who were watching. They ran out of the room like a heard of scared cattle. If they had stayed, they would have been cealing there fate of getting hit by one of my marbles. Sadly, no one saw me receive my medel for winning the game.

_____   _____

_____   _____

_____   _____

_____   _____

_____   _____

_____   _____

_____   _____

Building Spelling Skills

WEEK 27

Spelling List

This Week's Focus:
- Spell words with easily confused spellings

STEP 1 Read and Spell

STEP 2 Copy and Spell

STEP 3 Cover and Spell

1. quiet
2. quite
3. angel
4. angle
5. already
6. all ready
7. desert
8. dessert
9. weather
10. whether
11. pitcher
12. picture
13. loose
14. lose
15. aisle
16. isle
17. dairy
18. diary
19. _____ bonus word
20. _____ bonus word

Word Meaning

Building Spelling Skills **WEEK 27**

Choose the correct words to fill in the blanks.

1. Please be _____. You are being _____ noisy.
    (quite, quiet)   (quite, quiet)

2. That's an _____ food cake. Did you measure the _____?
    (angle, angel)   (angle, angel)

3. I've _____ been there. We are _____ to go.
    (all ready, already)   (all ready, already)

4. I love to eat _____. Let's visit the _____.
    (dessert, desert)   (dessert, desert)

5. We're discussing _____ the _____ will clear up.
    (whether, weather)   (whether, weather)

6. Please pass the _____ of water. My _____ is in my wallet.
    (picture, pitcher)   (picture, pitcher)

7. The dog was _____. I don't want to _____ my dog.
    (loose, lose)   (loose, lose)

8. I walked down the _____. I was on a desert _____.
    (isle, aisle)   (isle, aisle)

9. I always take my _____ with me. I work in a _____.
    (diary, dairy)   (diary, dairy)

My Spelling Dictation

Write the sentences. Circle the spelling words.

1. _____

    _____

2. _____

    _____

Word Study

Building Spelling Skills

WEEK 27

Circle the word that matches the definition.

1. not noisy — quiet / quite
2. a sharp corner — angel / angle
3. by that time — already / all ready
4. a very dry place — desert / dessert
5. what it's like outside — weather / whether
6. a photograph or drawing — pitcher / picture
7. not tight — loose / lose
8. open space between shelves — aisle / isle
9. a book you write in — dairy / diary

Match syllables to make spelling words.
Write the complete words on the lines.

1. al — gel — 1. _____
2. pit — cher — 2. _____
3. des — er — 3. _____
4. an — ready — 4. _____
5. wheth — ert — 5. _____
6. weath — er — 6. _____
7. qui — sert — 7. _____
8. an — et — 8. _____
9. des — gle — 9. _____

Building Spelling Skills, Daily Practice • EMC 6684 © Evan-Moor Corporation

Edit for Spelling

Building Spelling Skills

Circle the words that are spelled correctly.

dairy	quiat	angle	wheather
quite	angal	desurt	picture
already	whether	lose	dessert
aile	picher	loose	isle

Circle the misspelled words in the sentences. Write them correctly on the lines.

1. The usher was dancing in the aile.
   _____

2. We listened to the wheather report to know weather we should travel.
   _____   _____

3. The pitchor was in the pictur.
   _____   _____

4. The daire farmer was all readi to milk his herd.
   _____   _____

5. I like to have it quit when I write in my diarry.
   _____   _____

6. We measured that angal alredy.
   _____   _____

7. The dessert is no place to eat your desert.
   _____   _____

8. Be careful not to loose your lose change.
   _____   _____

9. The angil was quit pretty.
   _____   _____

Building Spelling Skills

WEEK 28

Spelling List

This Week's Focus:
- Spell words with the suffixes -**less**, -**ful**, and -**ness**
- Spell words with the ending -**ly**

STEP 1 Read and Spell

STEP 2 Copy and Spell

STEP 3 Cover and Spell

1. hopeless
2. careless
3. homeless
4. tireless
5. hopeful
6. fearful
7. cheerful
8. careful
9. graceful
10. happily
11. friendly
12. angrily
13. swiftly
14. suddenly
15. darkness
16. goodness
17. sadness
18. kindness
19. _____ bonus word
20. _____ bonus word

Word Meaning

Fill in the blanks with spelling words.

1. You don't need to be _____ of the _____ gazelle.

2. It is never _____ to help the _____ find a place to sleep.

3. The mother was _____ not to step on her child's toes.

4. The store clerk was always _____ when greeting a customer.

5. I wish there was more _____ and _____ in the world.

6. To everyone's surprise, the sound _____ stopped.

7. I was _____ that I could visit my friend.

8. The deer ran _____ through the forest.

My Spelling Dictation

Write the sentences. Circle the spelling words.

1. _____

_____

2. _____

_____

Word Study

Add a suffix or ending to make spelling words.

> less   ful   ness   ly

1. hope   __hopeful__
2. hope   _____
3. sad   _____
4. friend   _____
5. tire   _____
6. fear   _____
7. cheer   _____
8. home   _____
9. grace   _____
10. happy   _____
11. care   _____
12. angry   _____
13. swift   _____
14. sudden   _____
15. dark   _____
16. good   _____
17. care   _____
18. kind   _____

Now circle the words above that required a change before adding the suffix or ending.

Divide these words into syllables.

1. hopeless   _____ _____
2. hopeful   _____ _____
3. darkness   _____ _____
4. angrily   _____ _____ _____
5. happily   _____ _____ _____
6. friendly   _____ _____
7. kindness   _____ _____

Edit for Spelling

Circle the 12 misspelled words below.
Write the words correctly on the lines.

There's Always Hope

Sudenly, there was darknes. I was carelass to let my flashlight go out while camping in the backyard. I sat fearfull about the strange noises coming from everywhere. I was hopefull I could find some batteries. I was tireles in my search, but I finally gave up. All seemed hopelass. Sadnuss filled my body.

When all seemed lost, a gracefil figure tiptoed up to my tent. A friendy face peeked inside. My mom was cheerfal when she asked, "Is everything all right out here?"

My worries vanished swifly, as my mom handed me a new package of batteries.

Building Spelling Skills

WEEK 29

Spelling List

This Week's Focus:
- Spell words with the prefixes **dis-**, **un-**, **re-**, and **mis-**

STEP 1 Read and Spell
STEP 2 Copy and Spell
STEP 3 Cover and Spell

1. disappear
2. disappoint
3. disagree
4. dishonest
5. unable
6. uncertain
7. unbeaten
8. uncomfortable
9. unkind
10. unknown
11. rewrite
12. review
13. rebuild
14. recall
15. misbehave
16. misuse
17. misunderstand
18. misspell
19. _____ bonus word
20. _____ bonus word

Building Spelling Skills, Daily Practice • EMC 6684

Word Meaning

Complete the crossword puzzle using spelling words.

Across
1. to make again
4. not known
5. uneasy
9. to look over again
10. not nice
11. to remember

Down
2. can't do
3. to argue
4. not sure
6. to spell wrong
7. to write again
8. to use incorrectly

My Spelling Dictation

Write the sentences. Circle the spelling words.

1. _____

2. _____

Word Study

Building Spelling Skills — WEEK 29

Add the correct prefix to the base word.
Write the word in the blank.

> dis   un   re   mis

1. The child was unhappy because he was _____ to ride the horse.
   _{able}

2. She couldn't _____ her friend's name.
   _{call}

3. You may get hurt if you _____ that tool.
   _{use}

4. I'm afraid I must _____ with your opinion.
   _{agree}

5. Did you _____ that word? Check the dictionary.
   _{spell}

6. Use nice paper to _____ your report.
   _{write}

7. The runner was happy to announce that she was _____
   _{beaten}
   in all of her races.

8. Because he was _____ his answer was correct, he thought
   _{certain}
   about it again.

9. The rainbow will soon _____.
   _{appear}

10. The princess thought the bed was _____.
    _{comfortable}

Edit for Spelling

Building Spelling Skills — WEEK 29

Circle the words that are spelled correctly.

disappear	disapoint	dishonest	uncomfortable
disagree	review	missbehave	mispell
unable	uncurtain	unknown	recall
unbeten	unkind	rebild	misunderstand

Circle the misspelled words in the sentences.
Write them correctly on the lines.

1. The magician didn't disapoint the audience. He made a rabbit disapear.

   _____   _____

2. Students can missunderstand the meaning of a word, especially when it is mispelled.

   _____   _____

3. I'm sure you won't disagre that it is bad to be dishonist.

   _____   _____

4. If I recal correctly, you often missbehave.

   _____   _____

5. Let's revew and rerite your notes so you will do better on the test.

   _____   _____

6. I always get uncomfortible when someone is being unkin.

   _____   _____

Building Spelling Skills

WEEK 30

Spelling List

This Week's Focus:
- Spell multisyllabic words

STEP 1 Read and Spell
STEP 2 Copy and Spell
STEP 3 Cover and Spell

1. multiply
2. imagination
3. favorite
4. computer
5. citizenship
6. invisible
7. undercover
8. enjoyment
9. discussion
10. America
11. unusual
12. example
13. melody
14. temperature
15. understanding
16. experiment
17. explanation
18. oxygen
19. _____ bonus word
20. _____ bonus word

Building Spelling Skills, Daily Practice • EMC 6684   120   © Evan-Moor Corporation

Word Meaning

Fill in the blanks with spelling words.

1. We had to adjust the _____ because everyone was cold.

2. My _____ thing is to use my creativity and _____ to write a story.

3. I get so much _____ from my new _____.

4. Every person in the United States of _____ should practice good _____.

5. My _____ of the game was better the second time.

6. The clever _____ agent tried to make himself _____ in the crowd.

7. She played an _____ _____ on her guitar.

8. Finding the area of a square is an _____ of when to _____.

My Spelling Dictation

Write the sentences. Circle the spelling words.

1. _____

_____

2. _____

_____

Word Study

Building Spelling Skills — WEEK 30

Write the spelling word that means the opposite of each word or phrase.

1. least-liked _____
2. visible _____
3. divide _____
4. typical _____

Divide these words into syllables.

1. multiply _____ _____ _____
2. favorite _____ _____ _____
3. enjoyment _____ _____ _____
4. temperature _____ _____ _____ _____ _____
5. oxygen _____ _____ _____
6. discussion _____ _____ _____
7. citizenship _____ _____ _____ _____
8. America _____ _____ _____ _____
9. unusual _____ _____ _____ _____
10. understanding _____ _____ _____ _____
11. explanation _____ _____ _____ _____
12. imagination _____ _____ _____ _____ _____

Edit for Spelling

Circle the 14 misspelled words below.
Write the words correctly on the lines.

My Friend the Computer Programmer

My friend, the computor programmer, has a great imagenation. For exampel, he has created programs that

- help students learn to multipi,
- explain how to practice good citisenship,
- give facts about the United States of Amereca, and
- help students write songs for a cyber rock band.

My friend is now working on two programs, an unusal action game and a cyber science experiment. The action game will have an invisable undorcover police officer as the hero. The experement will help students with their undurstanding of oxigen and tempurature. He hopes both programs will bring injoyment to many students.

_____ _____

_____ _____

_____ _____

_____ _____

_____ _____

_____ _____

_____ _____

My Spelling Tests

Using Your Spelling Test Forms:

First

Use the following pages for your Friday spelling tests. Write your answers on these forms.

Then

Record your score on your spelling record form on pages 156 and 157.

Spelling Test

Building Spelling Skills — WEEK 1

Listen to the words.
Write each word on a line.

1. _____
2. _____
3. _____
4. _____
5. _____
6. _____
7. _____
8. _____
9. _____
10. _____

11. _____
12. _____
13. _____
14. _____
15. _____
16. _____
17. _____
18. _____
19. _____
20. _____

Listen to the sentences.
Write them on the lines.

1. _____
   _____
   _____

2. _____
   _____
   _____

Spelling Test

Building Spelling Skills — WEEK 2

Listen to the words.
Write each word on a line.

1. _____
2. _____
3. _____
4. _____
5. _____
6. _____
7. _____
8. _____
9. _____
10. _____
11. _____
12. _____
13. _____
14. _____
15. _____
16. _____
17. _____
18. _____
19. _____
20. _____

Listen to the sentences.
Write them on the lines.

1. _____
_____
_____

2. _____
_____
_____

Spelling Test

Building Spelling Skills — WEEK 3

Listen to the words.
Write each word on a line.

1. _____
2. _____
3. _____
4. _____
5. _____
6. _____
7. _____
8. _____
9. _____
10. _____

11. _____
12. _____
13. _____
14. _____
15. _____
16. _____
17. _____
18. _____
19. _____
20. _____

Listen to the sentences.
Write them on the lines.

1. _____
   _____
   _____

2. _____
   _____
   _____

Building Spelling Skills, Daily Practice • EMC 6684   128   © Evan-Moor Corporation

Spelling Test

Building Spelling Skills — WEEK 4

Listen to the words.
Write each word on a line.

1. _____
2. _____
3. _____
4. _____
5. _____
6. _____
7. _____
8. _____
9. _____
10. _____

11. _____
12. _____
13. _____
14. _____
15. _____
16. _____
17. _____
18. _____
19. _____
20. _____

Listen to the sentences.
Write them on the lines.

1. _____
   _____
   _____

2. _____
   _____
   _____

Spelling Test

Building Spelling Skills

WEEK 5

Listen to the words.
Write each word on a line.

1. _____
2. _____
3. _____
4. _____
5. _____
6. _____
7. _____
8. _____
9. _____
10. _____

11. _____
12. _____
13. _____
14. _____
15. _____
16. _____
17. _____
18. _____
19. _____
20. _____

Listen to the sentences.
Write them on the lines.

1. _____
_____
_____

2. _____
_____
_____

Spelling Test

Building Spelling Skills — WEEK 6

Listen to the words.
Write each word on a line.

1. _____
2. _____
3. _____
4. _____
5. _____
6. _____
7. _____
8. _____
9. _____
10. _____

11. _____
12. _____
13. _____
14. _____
15. _____
16. _____
17. _____
18. _____
19. _____
20. _____

Listen to the sentences.
Write them on the lines.

1. _____
_____
_____

2. _____
_____
_____

Spelling Test

Building Spelling Skills — WEEK 7

Listen to the words.
Write each word on a line.

1. _____
2. _____
3. _____
4. _____
5. _____
6. _____
7. _____
8. _____
9. _____
10. _____

11. _____
12. _____
13. _____
14. _____
15. _____
16. _____
17. _____
18. _____
19. _____
20. _____

Listen to the sentences.
Write them on the lines.

1. _____
   _____
   _____

2. _____
   _____
   _____

Spelling Test

Building Spelling Skills — WEEK 8

Listen to the words.
Write each word on a line.

1. _____
2. _____
3. _____
4. _____
5. _____
6. _____
7. _____
8. _____
9. _____
10. _____

11. _____
12. _____
13. _____
14. _____
15. _____
16. _____
17. _____
18. _____
19. _____
20. _____

Listen to the sentences.
Write them on the lines.

1. _____
_____
_____

2. _____
_____
_____

Spelling Test

Building Spelling Skills — WEEK 9

Listen to the words.
Write each word on a line.

1. _____
2. _____
3. _____
4. _____
5. _____
6. _____
7. _____
8. _____
9. _____
10. _____

11. _____
12. _____
13. _____
14. _____
15. _____
16. _____
17. _____
18. _____
19. _____
20. _____

Listen to the sentences.
Write them on the lines.

1. _____
   _____
   _____

2. _____
   _____
   _____

Spelling Test

Building Spelling Skills — WEEK 10

Listen to the words.
Write each word on a line.

1. _____
2. _____
3. _____
4. _____
5. _____
6. _____
7. _____
8. _____
9. _____
10. _____

11. _____
12. _____
13. _____
14. _____
15. _____
16. _____
17. _____
18. _____
19. _____
20. _____

Listen to the sentences.
Write them on the lines.

1. _____
   _____
   _____
2. _____
   _____
   _____

Spelling Test

Listen to the words.
Write each word on a line.

Building Spelling Skills — WEEK 11

1. _____
2. _____
3. _____
4. _____
5. _____
6. _____
7. _____
8. _____
9. _____
10. _____

11. _____
12. _____
13. _____
14. _____
15. _____
16. _____
17. _____
18. _____
19. _____
20. _____

Listen to the sentences.
Write them on the lines.

1. _____
   _____
   _____

2. _____
   _____
   _____

Spelling Test

Building Spelling Skills — WEEK 12

Listen to the words.
Write each word on a line.

1. _____
2. _____
3. _____
4. _____
5. _____
6. _____
7. _____
8. _____
9. _____
10. _____

11. _____
12. _____
13. _____
14. _____
15. _____
16. _____
17. _____
18. _____
19. _____
20. _____

Listen to the sentences.
Write them on the lines.

1. _____
   _____
   _____

2. _____
   _____
   _____

Spelling Test

Building Spelling Skills — WEEK 13

Listen to the words.
Write each word on a line.

1. _____
2. _____
3. _____
4. _____
5. _____
6. _____
7. _____
8. _____
9. _____
10. _____

11. _____
12. _____
13. _____
14. _____
15. _____
16. _____
17. _____
18. _____
19. _____
20. _____

Listen to the sentences.
Write them on the lines.

1. _____
   _____
   _____

2. _____
   _____
   _____

Spelling Test

Building Spelling Skills — WEEK 14

Listen to the words.
Write each word on a line.

1. _____
2. _____
3. _____
4. _____
5. _____
6. _____
7. _____
8. _____
9. _____
10. _____

11. _____
12. _____
13. _____
14. _____
15. _____
16. _____
17. _____
18. _____
19. _____
20. _____

Listen to the sentences.
Write them on the lines.

1. _____
   _____
   _____

2. _____
   _____

Spelling Test

Building Spelling Skills — WEEK 15

Listen to the words.
Write each word on a line.

1. _____
2. _____
3. _____
4. _____
5. _____
6. _____
7. _____
8. _____
9. _____
10. _____

11. _____
12. _____
13. _____
14. _____
15. _____
16. _____
17. _____
18. _____
19. _____
20. _____

Listen to the sentences.
Write them on the lines.

1. _____
   _____
   _____

2. _____
   _____
   _____

Spelling Test

Building Spelling Skills — WEEK 16

Listen to the words.
Write each word on a line.

1. _____
2. _____
3. _____
4. _____
5. _____
6. _____
7. _____
8. _____
9. _____
10. _____

11. _____
12. _____
13. _____
14. _____
15. _____
16. _____
17. _____
18. _____
19. _____
20. _____

Listen to the sentences.
Write them on the lines.

1. _____
   _____
   _____

2. _____
   _____
   _____

Spelling Test

Building Spelling Skills — WEEK 17

Listen to the words.
Write each word on a line.

1. _____
2. _____
3. _____
4. _____
5. _____
6. _____
7. _____
8. _____
9. _____
10. _____

11. _____
12. _____
13. _____
14. _____
15. _____
16. _____
17. _____
18. _____
19. _____
20. _____

Listen to the sentences.
Write them on the lines.

1. _____
_____
_____

2. _____
_____
_____

Spelling Test

Building Spelling Skills — WEEK 18

Listen to the words.
Write each word on a line.

1. _____
2. _____
3. _____
4. _____
5. _____
6. _____
7. _____
8. _____
9. _____
10. _____

11. _____
12. _____
13. _____
14. _____
15. _____
16. _____
17. _____
18. _____
19. _____
20. _____

Listen to the sentences.
Write them on the lines.

1. _____
   _____

2. _____
   _____
   _____

Spelling Test

Building Spelling Skills **WEEK 19**

Listen to the words.
Write each word on a line.

1. _____
2. _____
3. _____
4. _____
5. _____
6. _____
7. _____
8. _____
9. _____
10. _____

11. _____
12. _____
13. _____
14. _____
15. _____
16. _____
17. _____
18. _____
19. _____
20. _____

Listen to the sentences.
Write them on the lines.

1. _____
_____

2. _____
_____
_____

Spelling Test

Building Spelling Skills — WEEK 20

Listen to the words.
Write each word on a line.

1. _____
2. _____
3. _____
4. _____
5. _____
6. _____
7. _____
8. _____
9. _____
10. _____

11. _____
12. _____
13. _____
14. _____
15. _____
16. _____
17. _____
18. _____
19. _____
20. _____

Listen to the sentences.
Write them on the lines.

1. _____
   _____

2. _____
   _____
   _____

Spelling Test

Building Spelling Skills — WEEK 21

Listen to the words.
Write each word on a line.

1. _____
2. _____
3. _____
4. _____
5. _____
6. _____
7. _____
8. _____
9. _____
10. _____

11. _____
12. _____
13. _____
14. _____
15. _____
16. _____
17. _____
18. _____
19. _____
20. _____

Listen to the sentences.
Write them on the lines.

1. _____
   _____
   _____

2. _____
   _____
   _____

Spelling Test

Building Spelling Skills — WEEK 22

Listen to the words.
Write each word on a line.

1. _____
2. _____
3. _____
4. _____
5. _____
6. _____
7. _____
8. _____
9. _____
10. _____

11. _____
12. _____
13. _____
14. _____
15. _____
16. _____
17. _____
18. _____
19. _____
20. _____

Listen to the sentences.
Write them on the lines.

1. _____
   _____
   _____

2. _____
   _____
   _____

Spelling Test

Building Spelling Skills — WEEK 23

Listen to the words.
Write each word on a line.

1. _____
2. _____
3. _____
4. _____
5. _____
6. _____
7. _____
8. _____
9. _____
10. _____

11. _____
12. _____
13. _____
14. _____
15. _____
16. _____
17. _____
18. _____
19. _____
20. _____

Listen to the sentences.
Write them on the lines.

1. _____
   _____
   _____

2. _____
   _____
   _____

Spelling Test

Building Spelling Skills — WEEK 24

Listen to the words.
Write each word on a line.

1. _____
2. _____
3. _____
4. _____
5. _____
6. _____
7. _____
8. _____
9. _____
10. _____
11. _____
12. _____
13. _____
14. _____
15. _____
16. _____
17. _____
18. _____
19. _____
20. _____

Listen to the sentences.
Write them on the lines.

1. _____
    _____
    _____

2. _____
    _____
    _____

Spelling Test

Building Spelling Skills — WEEK 25

Listen to the words.
Write each word on a line.

1. _____
2. _____
3. _____
4. _____
5. _____
6. _____
7. _____
8. _____
9. _____
10. _____

11. _____
12. _____
13. _____
14. _____
15. _____
16. _____
17. _____
18. _____
19. _____
20. _____

Listen to the sentences.
Write them on the lines.

1. _____
_____

2. _____
_____

Spelling Test

Listen to the words.
Write each word on a line.

1. _____
2. _____
3. _____
4. _____
5. _____
6. _____
7. _____
8. _____
9. _____
10. _____

11. _____
12. _____
13. _____
14. _____
15. _____
16. _____
17. _____
18. _____
19. _____
20. _____

Listen to the sentences.
Write them on the lines.

1. _____
_____
_____

2. _____
_____
_____

Spelling Test

Building Spelling Skills — WEEK 27

Listen to the words.
Write each word on a line.

1. _____
2. _____
3. _____
4. _____
5. _____
6. _____
7. _____
8. _____
9. _____
10. _____

11. _____
12. _____
13. _____
14. _____
15. _____
16. _____
17. _____
18. _____
19. _____
20. _____

Listen to the sentences.
Write them on the lines.

1. _____
   _____

2. _____
   _____

Building Spelling Skills, Daily Practice • EMC 6684   © Evan-Moor Corporation

Spelling Test

Building Spelling Skills — WEEK 28

Listen to the words.
Write each word on a line.

1. _____
2. _____
3. _____
4. _____
5. _____
6. _____
7. _____
8. _____
9. _____
10. _____

11. _____
12. _____
13. _____
14. _____
15. _____
16. _____
17. _____
18. _____
19. _____
20. _____

Listen to the sentences.
Write them on the lines.

1. _____
   _____

2. _____
   _____
   _____

Spelling Test

Building Spelling Skills — WEEK 29

Listen to the words.
Write each word on a line.

1. _____
2. _____
3. _____
4. _____
5. _____
6. _____
7. _____
8. _____
9. _____
10. _____

11. _____
12. _____
13. _____
14. _____
15. _____
16. _____
17. _____
18. _____
19. _____
20. _____

Listen to the sentences.
Write them on the lines.

1. _____
   _____
   _____

2. _____
   _____
   _____

Spelling Test

Listen to the words.
Write each word on a line.

1. _____
2. _____
3. _____
4. _____
5. _____
6. _____
7. _____
8. _____
9. _____
10. _____

11. _____
12. _____
13. _____
14. _____
15. _____
16. _____
17. _____
18. _____
19. _____
20. _____

Listen to the sentences.
Write them on the lines.

1. _____
_____

2. _____
_____

My Spelling Record

Building Spelling Skills

Week	Date	Number Correct	Words Missed
1			
2			
3			
4			
5			
6			
7			
8			
9			
10			
11			
12			
13			
14			
15			

My Spelling Record

Building Spelling Skills

Week	Date	Number Correct	Words Missed
16			
17			
18			
19			
20			
21			
22			
23			
24			
25			
26			
27			
28			
29			
30